Sheol & I

Their Meaning and Usage in the Word of God.

By

E. W. Bullinger, D.D.

ISBN: 978-1-78364-553-4

www.obt.org.uk

Unless indicated otherwise Scripture quotations are from The Authorized (King James) Version. Rights in the Authorized Version in the United Kingdom are vested in the Crown. Reproduced by permission of the Crown's patentee, Cambridge University Press.

****

THE OPEN BIBLE TRUST
Fordland Mount, Upper Basildon,
Reading, RG8 8LU, UK

Sheol & Hades

Their Meaning and Usage in the Word of God.

Contents

Page
5	Introduction
9	*Sheol*
13	All the occurrences of *sheol* in the Old Testament
21	*Hades*
27	Psalm 12
28	Psalm 12:6
35	All the occurrences of *hades* in the New Testament
37	Matthew 11:23
39	Matthew 16:18
41	Luke 10:15
43	Luke 16:23
45	Acts 2:27
47	Acts 2:31
49	1 Corinthians 15:55
51	Revelation 1:18
53	Revelation 6:8
55	Revelation 20:13
57	Revelation 20:14
59	Also on this Subject
63	About the Author
64	Bullinger's Last Book
66	Also by Bullinger
69	Further Reading
71	About this Book

Introduction

Introduction

Few words call for more careful study than the Hebrew *"Sheol,"* and its Greek equivalent *"Hades."*

And few words are more obscured in our English Versions of the Bible because of the various ways in which they are treated in Translation.

The two words are different in their sources, while they are identical in their use in Holy Scripture.

Sheol is peculiarly a word of Divine Origin. It belongs to the Hebrew Bible, and is coined, so to speak, by the Holy Spirit Himself. It can be understood, therefore only by observing the way in which He has used it; learning there from the meaning which He has Himself given it.

With the Greek word, *Hades,* it is different. It is used, in the New Testament, to represent the Old Testament word *Sheol.* But *Hades* is a Greek word, and it had a history, and a meaning long before it was used by the Holy Spirit. It comes to us with all its associations in Greek literature, and its connection with heathen Mythology. It comes pervaded and permeated with all its heathen traditions. But the moment the Holy Spirit takes it up and uses it, all these are discarded, and set forever aside. Henceforth it can mean in the New Testament only what its Hebrew equivalent (*Sheol*) means in the Old Testament.

The Holy Spirit has, in doing this, "purified" it (in accordance with Ps. 12:6). Whatever *Sheol* means in the Old Testament, that

Hades means in the New Testament. In Greek works, of course, it still bears the meaning the Greeks put upon it; but *that meaning has no place in Scripture.*

It matters not, therefore, what Heathen "Mythology may have imagined; or what Tradition has handed down; what man may say; or what we may think. There is only one question: and that is a matter of supreme importance – What does God say about it; and How does the Holy Spirit use it in the Word of God?

If we know this we know *all that can be known*. No one can get beyond this. If, therefore, we put our readers in possession of the facts, they will have all the evidence before them, and be independent of all earthly and human teachers.

Sheol

Sheol

This Hebrew word *Sheol*, about which there is so much misunderstanding and controversy, occurs *sixty-five* times in the Old Testament. We propose to give the list, complete from the A.V., with the R.V. variations; calling attention to the fact that the American R.V. does not translate the word at all, but simply transliterates it thus: "Sheol".

To enable the eye to help the understanding, we have given the three renderings in three different types; and have referred to the R.V. text and margin in the notes. In all cases where not otherwise noted, the R.V. text is the same as the A.V.

The variations are indicated as follows:

* R.V. marg., Heb. *Sheol*. † R. V. pit; marg., Heb. *Sheol*. R. V. Sheol.	‖ R. V.: Sheol; marg., Or, *grave*. § R.V. marg., Or, *the grave;* Heb., *Sheol*. ** R.V. hell; marg., Heb. *Sheol*.

All the occurrences of the word *Sheol* in the Old Testament

All the occurrences of the word *Sheol* in the Old Testament

1. Gen. 37:35,† I will go down into **the grave**[1]
2. Gen. 42:38,* then shall ye bring down my grey hairs with sorrow to **the grave.**
3. Gen. 44:29,* with sorrow to **the grave.**
4. Gen. 44:31,* with sorrow to **the grave.**
5. Num. 16:30,* they go down quick into the PIT.
6. Num. 16:33,* they went down alive into the PIT.
7. Deut. 32:22, † shall burn unto the lowest *hell.*
8. 1 Sam. 2:6,* He bringeth down to **the grave.**
9. 2 Sam. 22:6,‡ the sorrows (R.V. cords) of *hell* compassed me.
10. 1 Kings 2:6,* let not his hoar head go down to **the grave** in peace.
11. 1 Kings 2:9,* his hoar head bring thou down to **the grave.**
12. Job 7:9,‖ he that goeth down to **the grave.**
13. Job 11:8,‖ deeper than *hell*; what canst thou know?
14. Job 14:13,‖ wouldest hide me in **the grave.**

---

[1] This being the first occurrence of the word *Sheol*, the R.V. gives this note in the margin: "Heb. *Sheol*, the name of the abode of the dead, answering to the Greek Hades, Acts 2:27." This note is altogether wrong. (1) It is *interpretation* and not *translation*. (2) It prejudges the word from the outset, fixing upon it the idea, "abode" which has a technical meaning applicable only to the living; thus anticipating the conclusion which cannot be arrived at until we have obtained all the evidence, and have it before us. (3) *Sheol* has nothing in it "answering to the Greek *Hades*." *Hades* must have the same meaning as *Sheol;* and must answer to that, and not to heathen Mythology. It must have the meaning which the Holy Spirit puts upon it, and not the meaning which the heathen had put on it.

15. Job 17:13,|| **the grave** is my house.
16. Job 17:16,|| they shall go down to the bars of the PIT.
17. Job 21:13,|| in a moment go down to **the grave**.
18. Job 24:19,|| so doth **the grave** [consume] those that have sinned.
19. Job 26:6,|| ***hell*** is naked before him.
20. Ps. 6:5,‡ in **the grave** who shall give thee thanks?
21. Ps. 9:17,*the wicked shall be turned (RV. returned) into ***hell***.
22. Ps. 16:10,‡ thou wilt not leave my soul in ***hell***.
23. Ps. 18:5,‡ the sorrows (R.V. cords) of ***hell*** compassed me.
24. Ps. 30:3,‡ thou hast brought up my soul from **the grave**.
25. Ps. 31:17,‡ let them be silent in **the grave**.
26. Ps. 49:14,‡ like sheep are they laid in **the grave**.
27. Ps. 49:14,‡ their beauty shall consume in **the grave**.
28. Ps. 49:15,‡ God will redeem my soul from the power of **the grave**.
29. Ps. 55:15,† let them go down quick into ***hell*** A.V. marg., **the grave**.)
30. Ps. 86:13,† thou hast delivered my soul from the lowest ***hell***. (A.V. marg., **the grave**.)
31. Ps. 88:3,|| my life draweth nigh unto **the grave**.
32. Ps. 89:48,|| shall he deliver his soul from the hand of **the grave**.
33. Ps. 116:3,|| the pains of ***hell*** gat hold upon me.
34. Ps. 139:8,‡ if I make my bed in ***hell*** thou art there.
35. Ps. 141:7,‡ our bones are scattered at **the grave's** mouth.
36. Prov. 1:12,|| let us swallow them up alive as **the grave**.
37. Prov. 5:5,|| her steps take hold on ***hell***.
38. Prov. 7:27,|| her house is the way to ***hell***.
39. Prov. 9:18,‡ her guests are in the depths of ***hell***.
40. Prov. 15:11,|| ***Hell*** and destruction are before the Lord.
41. Prov. 15:24,|| that he may depart from ***hell*** beneath.

42. Prov. 23:14,|| and shalt deliver his soul from *hell*.
43. Prov. 27:20,‡ *Hell* and destruction are never full.
44. Prov. 30:16,* **the grave**; and the barren womb.
45. Ecc. 9:10,* no device, nor knowledge in **the grave**.
46. Song 8:6, § jealousy is cruel as **the grave**.
47. Isa. 5:14, § *hell* hath enlarged herself.
48. Isa. 14:9, § *hell* from beneath is moved for thee. (A.V. marg., **the grave**.)
49. Isa.14:11, ** thy pomp is brought down to the **grave**.
50. Isa. 14:15, * thou shalt be brought down to *hell*.
51. Isa. 28:15, * with *hell* are we at agreement.
52. Isa. 28:18, * your agreement with *hell* shall not stand.
53. Isa. 38:10, * I shall go to the gates of **the grave**.
54. Isa. 38:14, * **the grave** cannot praise thee.
55. Isa. 57:9, * and didst debase thyself even unto *hell*.
56. Ezek. 31:15, ** he went down to **the grave**.
57. Ezek. 31:16, * I cast him down to *hell*.
58. Ezek. 31:17, * they also went down into *hell*.
59. Ezek. 32:21, * shall speak to him out of the midst of *hell*.
60. Ezek. 32:27, * are gone down to *hell* with their weapons.
61. Hos. 13:14, * I will ransom them from **the grave**.
62. Hos. 13:14* **O grave**, I will be thy destruction.
63. Amos 9:2, * though they dig into *hell*.
64. Jonah 2:2, out of the belly of *hell* cried I. (A.V. marg. **The grave**.)
65. Hab. 2:5, who enlargeth his desire as *hell*.

On a careful examination of the above list, we are almost bewildered with what looks like an utter absence of any settled plan or principle in the translation of the word *sheol*; in either the A.V. or R.V.

The American R.V. is alone consistent with itself, as it preserves the word *sheol*, uniformly, in each case.

Not only are three renderings used in the other two versions; but they are used almost at random. Now, one is in the text and another is in the margin; then, one is in the margin and another in the text.

If the confusion be so great with the Translators, how much more must it be so with the English readers?

The confusion will be further seen from the following Analysis:

Sheol is rendered

In the Text,	by the grave	31 times
	hell	31 times
	pit	3 times
		65 times in all

In the Margin "the grave" is put 4 times for "hell," thus neutralizing 4 passages, by reducing the total of "hell" renderings to 27, and correspondingly raising the total of "the grave" renderings to 35 instances out of 65.

We leave the Analysis of the R.V. renderings to our readers; and go on to call attention to a few points which stand out clearly in studying the above list.

1. It will be observed that in a majority of cases *Sheol* is rendered "the grave." To be exact, 54%: while "hell" is 41.5%; and "pit" only 4.5%.

    The grave, therefore, stands out on the face of the above list as the best and commonest rendering.

2. With regard to the word "pit," it will be observed that in each of the three cases where it occurs (Num. 16:30, 33; and Job 17:16), *the grave* is so evidently meant, that we may at once substitute that rendering, and banish "pit" from our consideration as a rendering of *Sheol*.

3. As to the rendering "hell," it does *not* represent *Sheol*; because both by Dictionary definition and by colloquial usage "hell" means the place of future *punishment*. *Sheol* has no such meaning; but denotes the *present condition of death*. "The grave" is, therefore, a far more suitable translation, because it visibly suggests to us what is invisible to the mind, *vis., the state of death*. It must, necessarily, be misleading to the English reader to see the former put to represent the latter.

4. The Student will find that "the grave," taken literally as well as figuratively, will meet all the requirements of the Hebrew *Sheol*: not that *Sheol* means so much specifically A grave, as generically THE Grave.

    Holy Scripture is all-sufficient to explain the word *Sheol* to us.

5. If we enquire of it in the above list of the occurrences of the word *Sheol*, it will teach:

    a. That, as to *direction*, it is down.
    b. That, as to *place*, it is in the earth.
    c. That, as to *nature*, it is put for *the state of death*. Not *death*, as the *act* of dying, for which we have no English word, but the *state*, or duration, or condition, of death. The Germans are more fortunate, having the word *sterbend* for the *act* of dying.

Sheol therefore means *the state of death*; or *the state of the dead*, of which *the grave* is a tangible evidence. It has to do only with the dead. It may sometimes be personified and represented as speaking as other inanimate things are. It may be represented by a coined word, *Grave-dom*, as meaning the dominion or power of *the grave*.

d. As to *relation*, it stands in *contrast* with the state of the living see Deut. 30:15, 19 and 1 Sam. 2:6-8. It is never once associated with the living, except by contrast.

e. As to *association*, it is used in connection with mourning (Gen. 37:34, 35), sorrow (Gen. 42:38, 2 Sam. 22:6, Ps. 18:5; 116:3), fright and terror (Num. 16:27, 34), weeping (Isa. 38:3, 10, 15, 20), silence (Ps. 31:17; 6:5; Ecc. 9:10), no knowledge (Ecc. 9:5, 6, 10), punishment (Num. 16:27, 34; 1 Kings 2:6, 9; Job 24:19; Ps. 9:17, R.V. RE-turned to the condition they were in before their resurrection).

f. And, finally, as to *duration*, the dominion of *Sheol* or the grave will continue until, and end only with, *resurrection*, which is the only exit from it (see Hos. 13:14, etc.; and compare Ps. 16:10 with Acts 2:27, 31; 13:35).

Our readers can follow out the further study of this important word for themselves: and can judge as to the correctness of the few conclusions we have drawn from the above list; and thus be established in God's truth.

Hades

Hades

Next to the Old Testament Hebrew word SHEOL, this New Testament Greek word, HADES is one of the most important.

Our present object and desire is to discover the way in which the Holy Spirit uses it; and to find out the sense in which He intends us to understand it. Apart from this, all our study of the word is useless.

It matters not what men may say, whether Pagan or Christian. Heathen Mythology, Human Tradition, and Christian Theology have no place in this study. They will lead us astray instead of guiding us: they will hinder us rather than help us.

The Old Testament has one advantage over the New. Its Hebrew words are the words of the Holy Spirit – and all knowledge of Hebrew starts with the Hebrew Bible. It is the fountain-head of that language; and there is no previous Hebrew literature behind it.

But when we come to the New Testament, the case is entirely different. Here, the Holy Spirit takes up *human words* which had been used among the Greeks for centuries, and had already acquired senses, and meanings, and usages; human in their development, as they were human in their origin.

It is this that marks the great difference between the languages of the Old and New Testaments. There is not only the difference between the two languages, as such; but the difference, also, as to their origin.

The Hebrew is, in this respect, Divine in its origin; the Greek is human. In the former case the Holy Spirit uses *His own* words in which to express His own revelation. In the latter case he takes *human* words, words pertaining to the earth. He uses "the tongues of men" and not "of angels" (1 Cor. 13:1; 2 Cor 12:4).

Now in "the tongues of men" there is this important phenomenon that, man, being a fallen creature, impresses that fact on the language he uses, as well as upon everything in which he comes into connection. He uses words conformable to his fallen condition. He has invented words to express his abominable sins; and words to express his filthy thoughts. Even words that *once* had a good meaning he has brought down to his own fallen level. This is true of all languages: but our examples may with advantage, be taken from our own language.

1. APOLOGY meant originally, *a defence*. Hence "Jewel's *Apology*" is the title of Bishop Jewel's *defence* of the Reformation. But inasmuch as man's defences are so often only *excuses*, the word has come to have almost the opposite meaning.

2. PREVENT meant to *precede* or *get before*. But, because, when one man gets before another, it is generally to oust him or hinder him, so the word has been lowered in its meaning, in order to correspond with this trait of man's fallen nature.

3. SIMPLE meant *honest, artless*; (lit., *without a fold*). But, because people who act on this principle in business, are, in this fallen world, looked upon as fools, so the word has come to mean *foolish*.

4. SILLY meant *innocent, inoffensive* (Ang. Sax. *Salig*). This is its meaning in 2 Tim. 3:6, "silly women." But, because such are looked on as an easy prey by false teachers, the word has come to mean weak and foolish.
5. STORY meant *a tale* or *history*. But because such are more often false than true, the word has fallen to its modern meaning of *untruth*.

6. CENSURE meant simply *judgment* or *reckoning*. But because such, when used on men, generally has to be adverse, so the word is not confined to *blame*.

And so we might go on to increase our list.[2] But the above will suffice to show the deterioration of words in their use by fallen man. It was the same in the Greek, and many examples could be given.

But our point is this: that man has made changes in his own language in the course of centuries, and has modified, and in many cases lowered and degraded, by his usage, the meanings of words.

This shows us the fallacy of judging New Testament Greek by Classical Greek. Those who do not know enough call the New Testament "bad Greek." But they do not allow for two facts. First, that while the words are Greek, the *idiom* is Hebrew: and Second, that these words are to be understood, not in their former classical sense, but in the sense in which they were

---

[2] Those who care to follow the subject out will find further examples in "impose," "vagabond," "impertinent," "wretch," "sottish," "inquisition," "imp," "craft," "knave," "subtle," "cunning," "charity," etc.

used in the time of our Lord; always excepting the cases where they are purified by the Holy Spirit.

For when He takes up human words and deigns to use them to make known Divine, Heavenly and Infinite truths, it is clear that He will do so in an absolutely perfect manner.

Consequently (i) there are very many Greek words that He *never uses* at all. (ii) There are words which He purifies, and uses in a *higher* sense than that in which the Greeks had ever before used them. (iii) there are words which He purifies and uses in a totally *different* sense, and (iv) there are Greek words which He Himself coined, which no man had ever used before, and which cannot be found in any human writings.

The Twelfth Psalm contains an important statement as to this difference between man's words and Jehovah's words; and of the necessity for the purification of the former before they could be used by the Lord.

This is shown, first by its Structure, which is as follows.

Psalm 12

```
A    | 1. Decrease of the good.
  B  | a | 2. Man's words (Vain, Flattering, Double).
     |   b | 3, 4 Their end. (Cut off."
     |       C | 5-. The oppression of the poor
     |           D | -5-. The sighing of the needy.
     |           D | -5-. The arising of the Lord.
     |       C | -5. The deliverance from oppression.
  B  | a | 6.   Jehovah's words. (Pure).
     |   b | 7. Their end. "Preserved."
A    | 8. Increase of the wicked.
```

The correspondence of these members is perfect and complete. But the important one is "B" (*vv.* 2-4), and "*B*" (*vv.* 6, 7), where the contrast is shown between Man's words and Jehovah's words. The former are declared to be "vanity," "flattering," and "double"; and are to be "cut off": while Jehovah's words are "pure," and are to be "preserved forever."

But there is more than this in verse 6. Not only are Jehovah's own words "pure" in themselves; but when He used earthly words, they had to be "purified" before He could use them.

There are one or two points to be noted in this verse in order to understand its lesson. There is no sense in the translation, "a furnace of earth." The R.V. renders this "a furnace upon the earth." But is surely is nothing to the point whether the furnace is made "of" earth or metal; or whether it is placed "upon" the earth or upon a stand.

The Hebrew preposition (*Lamed*) means *to*, and is frequently used of *possession* or *pertaining to*,[3] and may be translated by the word "of" or "belonging unto."[4]

Then verse 6 will read thus, in four alternate parallel lines; the first and third of which relate to *words*; whilst the second and fourth lines relate to *purification*.

Psalm 12:6.

```
a | c | The words of the Lord are pure words.
        d | As silver tried in a furnace.
    c | [Words] belonging to the earth.
        d | Purified seven times.
```

Here, we see that Jehovah's words *are* pure in themselves. But the words of this world have to be *made* pure; yea, with a great purification, seven times repeated – or Divine and Spiritually perfect – process.

Now we can return to our statement, made above, and watch this purifying process as the great Refiner carries out His wonderful but necessary work.

ii. Some words (as we said above) He uses in a *higher* sense: *e.g.,*

---

[3] Gen. 31:1, "all that was to our father:" *i.e.,* all that was our father's. So 29:9; 47:4. So frequently we have "a Psalm of David," *lit.,* to David, *i.e.,* David's, by or belonging to David (Ps. 3; 4; 25; 26; 27).

[4] See 1 Kings 15:31, "the chronicles of the Kings of Israel"; Ruth 2:3, "the field of Boaz," which is rendered "belonging unto Boaz."

1. *(arete)*. Man used this only of *manhood* or *manly prowess*. But the Holy Spirit uses it in the far higher sense of Divine *glory* (Hab. 3:3), and *praise* (Isa. 42:8, 12; 43:21; 63:7). So also the only occurrences in the New Testament: Phil. 4:8; 1 Pet. 2:9; 2 Pet. 1:3, 5.

2. *(ethos)* was used only of the *haunt* of an animal; but in the New Testament it is used of moral custom or character (1 Cor. 15:33).

iii. Some words are used in a *different* sense: *e.g.,*

1. *(choregeo)* meant simply *to supply* or *furnish a chorus*. But the Spirit uses it of the Divine supply of all his people's needs (1 Pet. 4:11).

2. *(ecclisea)* was used, by the Greeks, only of *a town's meeting* of its citizens (Acts 19:39). But the Spirit uses it of the assemblies of God's elect.

3. *(parakletos)* was used only of a *legal assistant* or *helper*. But Christ uses it of the Holy Spirit or "Comforter" within us that we may *not* sin (John 14:16, 26; 15:26; 16:7). And the Spirit uses it of Christ as the Advocate with the Father if we *do* sin (1 John 2:1).

4. *(scandalon)* was used only of a snare to catch animals; but in the New Testament it is used in a moral and spiritual sense of that which causes anyone to stumble or fall (Matt. 11:6); a sense in which the Greeks *never* used it.

iv. Some words were coined by the Inspiring Spirit, and are never found in the work of any Greek author, *e.g.,*

1. (*scandalizo*), *to cause to stumble* or *fall; to give cause of offence.*

2. (*epiousios*), in "the Lord's Prayer" rendered "daily"; but etymologically can be rendered only *coming upon* (*i.e., descending on us*, like the manna, *daily*); or *going upon* (*i.e.* for our going upon or journeying. [5]

Now, when we come to the study of the Greek word Hades we are confronted with the fact that it had already been in use by the Greeks for some centuries; and was, of course used in harmony with their Mythological Traditions.
Idolatry was not an evil into which man gradually fell. It was a gigantic masterpiece of Satan, having its seat of origin and development at Babylon. It was a perversion of primitive truth, and passed thence through the Greeks into Judaism, and thence into Romanism.

Hades became the embodiment of Satan's lie, "ye shall not surely die." Hence, *Hades* was used of the world of *darkness*, or the *spirit-world*; used indeed in much the same sense as Spiritists use it today.

The question, whether this is the sense in which the Holy Spirit desires us to understand the word, is therefore one of the first importance.

Heathen Mythologists, Jewish and Christian Traditionists, Romanists, and Spiritists all agree in answering "Yes."

---

[5] See paper on "the Lord's Prayer" in *Things to Come*, Vol. 12, 1906. Also *Figures of Speech* by the same author; page 73.

But we answer without hesitation or doubt, NO! And there is one great proof that settles it. In Acts 2:27, 31 it is used by the Holy Spirit as the substitute for *Sheol* in the quotation of Ps. 16:10. *Hades* must therefore mean in Acts what *Sheol* means in the Psalm.

The word comes into the New Testament, therefore, not from the Classical Greek, but through the Septuagint and the Hebrew of the Old Testament. And we are prepared to see it purified, by the Great Refiner, from all Pagan Mythology, Human Tradition, Romish corruption and Spiritist perversion.

When the Holy Spirit used it as the equivalent of His own word *Sheol* He settled, once for all, the sense in which He wishes us to understand it.

We are now in a position to continue our study of this Greek word.

We have seen above that, when the Holy Spirit took up *human* words, and used the words belonging to the earth, He purified them, like as silver is tried in a furnace, "purified seven times."

This word "*Hades*" was used by the Greeks in much the same sense as Romanists use the word Purgatory. But the question is, Is the word *Hades* used in the New Testament in the heathen sense which it had in the Greek Mythology? We answer, *undoubtedly it is not*. Christian Traditionists may prefer the Babylonian-Romish-Spiritist meaning: we prefer, and are content with, the Bible meaning as it is used by the Spirit of God.

The one fact that it is used in Acts 2:27, 31 (compare 13:30-37) as a substitute and equivalent for the word *Sheol* in Psalm 16:10, shows that it must be taken in the same sense in the New

Testament as the Hebrew Old Testament word *Sheol*; and not in the corrupt sense which heathen tradition had given it.

The only way to learn what this Bible-word *Hades* means; and the only way to arrive at the sense in which the Holy Spirit used it, is to study each place where He has used it. From this alone can we learn. Lexicons are useless; man's imaginations are worthless; his traditions are valueless; his theology is of no avail; his translations are without Divine authority. One thing, and only one thing, is necessary, and that is to find out what God says, and demand a "thus saith the Lord."

Discarding, therefore, everything outside the Word of God, we note,

> (1) That the Greek word *Hades* occurs *eleven* times in the New Testament. As the occurrences are so few, we shall be able to examine each passage in detail; as we were not able to do in the large number (65) of the occurrences of the Hebrew word *Sheol*.
> (2) In the A.V. this word is rendered ten times "hell," and once "grave" (1 Cor. 15:15). This has the marginal alternative "hell," while in Rev. 20:13, the Text "hell" has "the grave" in the margin.
> (3) In the R.V., and in the American R.V., every one of these passages is rendered uniformly "*Hades*" without any alternative rendering in the margin.

All the occurrences of Hades in the New Testament

All the occurrences of Hades in the New Testament

1. Matt. 11:23. "And thou Capernaum, shalt be brought down to **hades**."
2. Matt. 16:18. "The gates of **hades** shall not prevail against it."
3. Luke 10:15. "And thou, Capernaum, . . . shalt be brought down to **hades**."
4. Luke 16:23. "And in **hades**."
5. Acts 2:27. "Thou wilt not leave my soul in **hades**."
6. Acts 2:31. "His soul was not left in **hades**."
7. 1 Cor. 15:55. "O **hades** (A.V. *grave*) where is thy victory."
8. Rev. 1:18. "I have the keys of death and of **hades**."
9. Rev. 6:8. "His name . . . was Death, and **hades** followed after him."
10. Rev. 20:13. "And death and **hades** (A.V. marg. Or, *the grave*) delivered up the dead."
11. Rev. 20:14. "And death and **hades** were cast into the lake of fire."

In our examination of "*Sheol*" we showed that *THE grave* (not *A grave*) was the only rendering which accurately represents the Hebrew word *Sheol*. As *Hades* is used by the Holy Spirit as the New Testament substitute for the Old Testament *Sheol* it follows that the same meaning must be given to *Hades* in the New Testament.

Our readers will see that there is not one of the eleven passages where this may not be done, with great advantage to the elucidation of the text, and to the understanding of its meaning. But before we do this, let us note an important principle laid down in the twentieth of the "Thirty-nine Articles of Religion."

> **It is not lawful . . . to . . . so expound one place of Scripture, that it be repugnant to another**.

This principle is true: because, as no one text *is* repugnant to others, then there is something amiss either as to the translation of it; or as to our understanding of it.

In this case it behooves us to examine it and see where the fault lies. The one must be understood and explained in the light of the many; the one apparently more difficult passage must be made clear by the others which are quite plain.

If this method be not possible, then the difficult passage must be left unsolved for the present, with the prayer that God will, in his own time, bestow the needed grace and light. But in no case must we allow that one difficult passage to disturb all the others which are clear; nor must we give need for a moment to any false teaching which Tradition may have founded upon its misunderstanding or perversion of that one passage, whether through ignorance or malice.

With these preliminary observations we will consider each passage in order.

1. Matt. 11:23

"And thou Capernaum . . . shall be brought down to Hades."

This suggests but one fact, viz., the terrible judgment pronounced by our Lord against Capernaum: once a flourishing town in Palestine, but now (in proof of the truth of this prophecy) known only by a few insignificant mounds in which the ruins are actually *buried*.

What or where *Hades* is, is not stated. The word "down" is the only guide as to direction.

Isa. 14:14, 15 sheds further light, especially if we place the two passages side by side, and put the words as they are in the original:-

Matt. 11:23	Isa. 14:14, 15
"And thou, Capernaum, which art exalted to heaven, shalt be brought down to *Hades*."	"I will ascend above the brightness of the clouds; yet shalt thou be brought down to *Sheol*, to the sides of the pit."

Here *Sheol* is explained, by a Synonym, "the sides of the pit" (Heb. *Bor*[6]).

---

[6] The Heb. (*bor*) is *a rock-hewn sepulcher* as in Ps. 28:1, 34:3; 88:5; Isa. 14:19. Our English, *bore*, is doubtless derived from it. It is rendered *cistern* 10 times; dungeon 10 times; *fountain*, once; *well*, 9 times; and *pit*, 42 times

This is an inspired and authoritative definition, and explains that *Sheol* means the place *bored* in the earth; in other words, *the grave*; and that Capernaum was to be brought down thither. Its proud and unbelieving inhabitants were buried in *the grave*; and its houses and buildings are now *buried* in ruins.

2. Matt. 16:18

"On this Rock will I build my Assembly, and the gates of *Hades* shall not prevail against it."

Leaving aside the meaning of the word *Ecclesia* or Assembly, we note that the word rendered "prevail" is exceedingly strong. It means to *prevail against* or *over*; to *overcome* and *vanquish*.

It occurs elsewhere only in Luke 23:23, where "the voices of them *prevailed* and Pilate gave sentence that it should be as they desired." They *prevailed* against Pilate; but, neither they nor the grave could prevail against Christ. He rose again from *Hades*, or *the grave*. He gained the victory over Death and *Hades*, and His Assembly will be conquerors too. They will one day shout, "*O Hades*, where is thy victory . . . Thanks be to God which giveth us the victory through Jesus Christ our Lord" (1 Cor. 15:55-57). This victory will be in Resurrection; and Resurrection will be the great and abiding proof that *Hades* will not prevail against "the dead in Christ;" even as it prevailed not against Him.

The expression "the gates of *Hades*" is further explained by reference to Isa. 38:10; Job 38:17; Ps. 9:13; 107:18.

3. Luke 10:15

Is the parallel of Matt. 11:23.

4. Luke 16:23[7]

"And in *Hades* he lift up his eyes."

Here we propose another punctuation. Not that there is the slightest difficulty if we take the words as they stand, and substitute "the grave" for "hell."

It is then merely a representation of dead people speaking in *the grave*, as in Isa. 14:9-20; and as trees are represented as speaking in the parable of Jotham (Judges 9:8-15). The punctuation, as we know, is absolutely human. In the Greek manuscripts there is no trace of any punctuation of any kind whatsoever. Nor is punctuation a matter of precedent, or of human authority of any kind. It is entirely a matter of the particular context, and of agreement with the general teaching of Scripture on the point in question.

Nor is the change we suggest made of our own imagination in order to support any theories of our own. It is adopted by the Vulgate translation,[8] which though not the original text, and of no authority as a Text, is yet evidence of a fact. It is punctuated in the same way by Tatian, *Diatessaron* (A.D. 170) and Marcion (A.D. 145); as well as in the Ancient Jerusalem Syriac Version. And the fact is that the first three words of verse 23, form instead, the last three words of verse 22: a full stop being placed after the word *Hades*; while the word "and" is treated by this as meaning "also." So that the whole sentence would read thus:-

---

[7] For more on this passage see *The Rich Man and Lazarus* by E W Bullinger and the book *The Rich Man and Lazarus* B William Campbell

[8] "Sepultus est in Inferno," *was buried in Hades.*

> "But the rich man also died, and was buried also in *Hades*."

"Buried also," implies what is only *inferred* as to Lazarus, meaning that the one was buried as well as the other. Whether this punctuation be allowed, or not, does not affect the matter in the slightest degree. For that is where *he was buried* in any case. It affects only the place where he is said to lift up his eyes.

This is further shown by the fact that the three verbs "died," "buried," and "he lift up," are not all in the same Tense as they appear to be from the English. The first two are in the past Tense, while the third is the present Participle, (*eparas*) *Lifting up*, thus commencing the 23rd verse with a new thought.

Those who interpret this passage as though *Hades* were a place of *life* instead of *death*, make it "repugnant" to every other place where the word occurs, and to many other scriptures which are *perfectly plain, e.g.,* Ps. 146:4; Ecc. 9:6, 10; Ps. 6:5; 31:17; 115:17.

In any case, all that is material to our study here, and now, is the one fact, that the rich man died, and was "buried also in *Hades*," *i.e.*, the grave.

5. Acts 2:27.

"Thou wilt not leave my soul (*i.e.*, me) in *Hades*."

6. Acts 2:31.

"His soul (*i.e.*, He) was not left in *Hades*."

These two passages, being respectively the quotation and interpretation of Ps. 16:10, must have the meaning that *Sheol* there has; and show that they speak "of the resurrection of Christ" (*v.* 31) from *the grave*. This is clear if we read the whole context, Acts 2:24-35; and 13:30-37. *Hades* is, here, the place where "corruption is seen; and "resurrection" is the only way of exit from it.

7. 1 Cor. 15:55.

"O *Hades*, where is thy victory."

This is translated in the A.V. "O grave," which is conclusive as to the meaning to be put upon the word *Hades*.[9]

Moreover, it is a quotation from Hos. 13:14, where the Hebrew is *Sheol*. The four lines in this verse are arranged as an introversion, where the first line corresponds with the fourth, and the second with the third. This shows that the word in 1 Cor. 15:55 must be *Hades*, and not "death."

a	I will ransom them from the power of **Sheol**;
b	I will redeem them from **death**;
b	O **death**, I will be thy plagues;
a	O **Sheol**, I will be thy destruction.

---

[9] The R.V. has a various reading which repeats the word (*thanate*) *O death*, and transposes the words "sting" and "victory." It is in this passage, therefore, neutral for our purpose.

8. Rev. 1:18

"I have the keys of *Hades* and death."

This must mean that, in virtue of Christ's resurrection, He has henceforth the power over death and *the grave*. Satan will one day be deprived of his power over death, which he now has, according to Heb. 2:14. When John sees Christ risen, not only from the dead, but risen up from His seat (Luke 13:25) for judgment in "the Day of the Lord" (Rev. 1:10), he hears this wondrous proclamation of Christ's power, and of His intention then to put forth that power and to use it.

9. Rev. 6:8.

"His name . . . was Death, and *Hades* followed with him."

The grave is that which follows after death. There, all will be buried who shall be the victims of this "death," or pestilence, here foretold and personified.

10. Rev. 20:13.

"And death and *Hades* (marg. *The grave*) delivered up the dead which were in them."

This teaches us that *Hades* contains, not living people, but "the dead" who "LIVED NOT AGAIN until the thousand years were finished" (see verse 5). This passage is clear; and we are to explain the other ten passages so that they be not "repugnant" to it.

11. Rev. 20:14.

"And death and *Hades* were cast into the lake of fire. This is the second death."

This verse tells of the time when *Hades* or *Sheol, i.e., the grave*, will no more exist; when the prophecy of Hos. 13:14, will be fulfilled.

Hades or the grave will no longer be needed, for the all sufficient reason given in Rev. 21:4, "there shall be no more death." Thus, for the last time, we learn what may be gathered from all the other passages: *viz.*, that

1. *Hades* is invariably connected with *death*; but never with life: always with *dead* people; but never with the *living*. All in *Hades* will "NOT LIVE AGAIN," until they are raised from the dead (Rev. 20:5). If they do not "live again" until after they are raised, it is perfectly clear that they *cannot be alive now*. Language is useless for the purposes of revelation when it is made to do away with the great and fundamental doctrine of the RESURRECTION which is the great fact that is being revealed.

2. That the English word "hell" by no means represents the Greek "*Hades*"; as we have seen that it does not give a correct idea of its Hebrew equivalent, "*Sheol*."

3. That *Hades* can mean only and exactly what *Sheol* means, *viz.*, the place where "corruption" is seen (Acts 2:31. Compare Acts 13:34-37); and from which resurrection is the only exit (Rev. 20:14).

In the face of this result of our examination we may well discard all man's ideas, imaginations and thoughts.

We are commanded to "Search the Scriptures" (John 5:39): and the word rendered "search" here[10] means to *trace out* as a lion or a hound traces its prey by the trail or scent. Hence, the only way to find out the true meaning of a word, is to track it and follow it in all its occurrences, with the one object of observing and noting how the Holy Spirit of truth Himself has used it.

This is what we have now done; for, only thus can we arrive at the real meaning of a word or words with "which the Holy Ghost teacheth:" only thus can we be delivered from the traditions of men which make the Word of God of none effect.

---

[10] (*ereunao*).

Also on this Subject

Also on this Subject

Asleep in Christ
by Helaine Burch

In this book the author encourages the reader to seriously enquire into the nature of mankind and to consider his destiny after death.

- Has man a 'soul' or is man a 'soul'?
- What is 'soul'?
- What happens to the 'soul' at death?
- What is 'death'?
- Why does man 'die'?
- What is 'spirit'?
- What is the place of 'resurrection'?
- What is 'hell'?
- What is the second death?

These, and many other questions, are discussed dispassionately. However, this book is written with the affirmation that the Bible is the inspired Word of God and, as such, is inerrant in its teaching on the most fundamental aspects of being human: living and dying, life and death.

Copies of *Asleep in Christ,*
are available from

www.obt.org.uk

and from

The Open Bible Trust,
Fordland Mount, Upper Basildon,
Reading, RG8 8LU, UK.

They also available as eBooks
from Amazon Kindle and Apple,
and as KDP paperbacks from Amazon.

About the Author

Ethelbert W. Bullinger D.D. (1837-1913) was a direct descendant of Heinrich Bullinger, the great Swiss reformer who carried on Zwingli's work after the latter had been killed in war.

E. W. Bullinger was brought up a Methodist but sang in the choir of Canterbury Cathedral in Kent. He trained for and became an Anglican (Episcopalian) minister before becoming Secretary of the Trinitarian Bible Society. He was a man of intense spirituality and made a number of outstanding contributions to biblical scholarship and broad-based evangelical Christianity.

Bullinger's Last Book

The Foundations of Dispensation Truth

Bullinger's last book, reflecting his mature views.

This is Bullinger's last book and is his definitive work on the subject of dispensationalism. It covers the ministries of ...

- the prophets,
- the Son of God,
- those that heard Christ, and
- the ministry of Paul, the Apostle to the Gentiles.

He comments on the Gospels and the Pauline epistles and has a lengthy section on the Acts of the Apostles, followed by one explaining why miraculous signs of the Acts period ceased.

This is a newly typeset book, well presented in an easy to read format.

Copies of *The Foundations of Dispensational Truth,* and of the books listed on the next pages, are available from

www.obt.org.uk

and from

The Open Bible Trust,
Fordland Mount, Upper Basildon,
Reading, RG8 8LU, UK.

They also available as eBooks
from Amazon Kindle and Apple,
and as KDP paperbacks from Amazon.

Also by Bullinger

The Two Natures in the Child of God

The Bible sees the Christian as having an 'old nature', inherited through generation from Adam, and a 'new nature', bestowed through regeneration by God.

The names and characteristics of each are many and various, including "the natural man" and "the old man" over against "the divine nature" and "the new man".

The conflict between the two natures is discussed with details of our responsibilities regarding each, and the ultimate end of the old and new natures. Finally, practical suggestions are made for dealing with the old nature.

Available as an eBook from Amazon and Apple and as a KDP paperback from Amazon.

The following is a selection of works by E W Bullinger published by The Open Bible Trust

The Transfiguration
The Knowledge of God
God's Purpose in Israel
The Prayers of Ephesians
The Lord's Day (Revelation 1:10)
The Rich Man and Lazarus
The Importance of Accuracy
Christ's Prophetic Teaching
The Resurrection of the Body
The Divine Names and Titles
The Spirits in Prison: 1 Peter 3:17-4:6
The Lesson of the Book of Job: The Oldest Lesson in the World
The Seven Sayings to the Woman at the Well
The Foundations of Dispensational Truth
The Christian's Greatest Need
Introducing the Church Epistles
The Two Natures in the Child of God
The Name of Jehovah in the Book of Esther
The Names and Order of the Books of the Old Testament
The Second Advent in Relation to the Jew
The Vision of Isaiah: Its Structure and Scope
The Importance of Accuracy: in the study of the Bible

More information about the above can be seen on www.obt.org.uk from where they can be ordered.

Further reading

Search magazine

For a free sample of
the Open Bible Trust's magazine Search,
please email

admin@obt.org.uk

or visit

www.obt.org.uk/search

About this Book

Sheol & Hades

Their Meaning and Usage in the Word of God.

The Hebrew *Sheol* and its Greek equivalent *Hades* require careful study as few words are more obscured in our English Versions of the Bible then these two. This is so because of the various ways in which they are treated in translation.

The two words have different etymologies, yet they are identical in their use in Holy Scripture.

Sheol belongs to the Hebrew Bible, and is coined, so to speak, by the Holy Spirit Himself. It can be understood only by observing the way in which He has used it in the Scriptures; learning from there the meaning which He has Himself given it.

However, the Greek *Hades* is different. It had a history and a meaning long before it was used by the Holy Spirit in the New Testament. *Hades* comes to us with all its associations in Greek literature and, in particular, its connection with heathen Mythology. It comes pervaded and permeated with all its heathen traditions. However, when we consider it in the New Testament, all of these must be discarded, and set forever aside.

In the New Testament, *Hades* is to represent the Old Testament word *Sheol*. Hence in New Testament it can mean only what its Hebrew equivalent (*Sheol*) means in the Old Testament.

In his usual through and detailed style the author does an excellent job in explaining and clarifying these two words, touching upon every occurrence of each in the Scriptures.

Publications of The Open Bible Trust must be in accordance with its evangelical, fundamental and dispensational basis. However, beyond this minimum, writers are free to express whatever beliefs they may have as their own understanding, provided that the aim in so doing is to further the object of The Open Bible Trust. A copy of the doctrinal basis is available on **www.obt.org.uk** or from:

THE OPEN BIBLE TRUST
Fordland Mount, Upper Basildon,
Reading, RG8 8LU, UK

Printed in Great Britain
by Amazon